What's On Your Plate?

Lunch

Ted and Lola Schaefer

Chicago, Illinois

Editorial: Patrick Catel, Rosie Gordon, and Melanie Waldron
Design: Philippa Jenkins,Lucy Owen, and John Walker
Picture Research: Melissa Allison
Production: Chloe Bloom

Printed and bound in China by South China Printing Company.

10 09 08 07 06
10 9 8 7 6 5 4 3 2 1

Library of Congress Cataloguing-in-Publication Data:
Schaefer, Lola M., 1950-
    Lunch / Lola and Ted Schaefer.
    p. cm. -- (Raintree Perspectives)
    (What's On Your Plate?)
    Includes bibliographical references and index.
    ISBN-13: 978-1-4109-2215-1 (library binding - hardcover)
    ISBN-13: 978-1-4109-2367-7 (pbk.)
    1. Luncheons. I. Schaefer, Ted, 1948- II. Title. III. Series.
    TX733.S 34 2006
    641.5'3--dc22

2005031486

Acknowledgements
The publishers would like to thank the following for permission to reproduce photographs:
pp. 18, 26, Corbis; **p.** 6, Corbis/Charles Gupton; **p.** 19, Corbis/Lester Lefkowitz; **p.** 14, Corbis/Lew Robertson; **p.** 16, Creatas; **p.** 5, Getty Images; **p.** 27, Getty Images/Photonica; **pp.** 4, 5, 9, 10, 12, 13, 20, 21, 23, 24, 28, 29, Harcourt Education Ltd/MM Studios; **p.** 22, Harcourt Education Ltd/Tudor Photography; **pp.** 17, 25, PhotoEdit; **p.** 15, PhotoEdit/David Young-Wolff; **p.** 7, PhotoEdit/Mark Richards; **p.** 5, Photolibrary.com

Cover photograph of a sandwich reproduced with permission of Getty Images/Stone/Chris Everard

The publishers would like to thank Dr Sarah Schenker for her assistance in the preparation of this book.

Every effort has been made to contact copyright holders of any material reproduced in this book. Any omissions will be rectified in subsequent printings if notice is given to the publishers.

Disclaimer

Dedicated to the memory of Lucy Owen

Contents

Any words appearing in bold, *like this*, are explained in the Glossary.

What Is Lunch?

Lunch is the meal you eat in the middle of the day. You probably don't need a clock to tell you that it is lunchtime. You have used all the **energy** from your breakfast and you feel hungry! Food is the fuel that keeps you going, and lunch gives you a new supply.

sandwich

tortilla

yogurt

vegetables

vegetable soup

fruit salad

chicken and rice

Did you eat one of these for lunch this week?

Crab salad, crackers, and fresh fruit are a favorite lunch in Trinidad.

In the UK, many children like a cheese sandwich, a bowl of tomato soup, and grapes.

People often eat flatbread and lentil dhal, with a glass of sweetened buttermilk called lassi (LAH-see) for lunch in India.

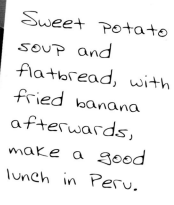

Sweet potato soup and flatbread, with fried banana afterwards, make a good lunch in Peru.

5

Why Do You Eat Lunch?

A healthy lunch gives your body the **nutrition** you need for the afternoon. Some foods help you grow and stay healthy, while others give you **energy** to play, work, or think.

The amount of energy in food is measured in **calories**. Different foods give your body different amounts of calories.

A good lunch will give you energy for the afternoon.

This chart shows some lunch foods and the amount of calories they supply.

Food	Serving	Calories
Vegetable soup	1 C	121
Whole grain crackers	10	85
Low-fat cottage cheese	1 C	170
Apple	1	65

C = ½ pint cups

6

Your body is using energy all the time, whether you are moving or sitting still. Activities that make you feel tired or out of breath use more calories. Running uses more energy than walking.

This bar chart is a guide to the amount of calories your body may use during these activities.

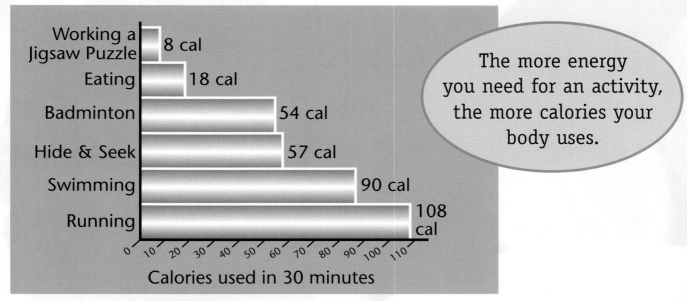

Working a Jigsaw Puzzle — 8 cal
Eating — 18 cal
Badminton — 54 cal
Hide & Seek — 57 cal
Swimming — 90 cal
Running — 108 cal

Calories used in 30 minutes

The more energy you need for an activity, the more calories your body uses.

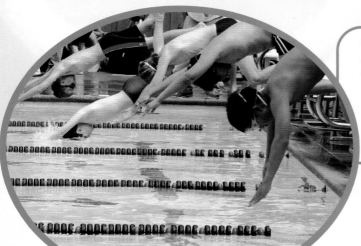

Quiz
How many calories would you use while swimming for one hour?

(Answer at the bottom of the page)

7

Answer: You would need 180 calories to swim for one hour.

What Are the Healthiest Lunch Foods?

The foods you choose for lunch can be part of a healthy **diet**. A diet is what you eat each day. A diet can be healthy or unhealthy because not all foods give you the same **nutrition**. You need to eat the right amounts of lots of different foods to give your body all of the **nutrients** it needs.

The food groups needed for a healthy diet are shown in this **food pyramid**.

GRAINS   VEGETABLES   FRUITS   FATS   DAIRY   MEAT & BEANS

How Much Do I Need?

A child of nine should eat the following amounts each day, including meals and snacks:

grains	vegetables	fruits	dairy	meat and beans
6 oz	2½ C	1½ C	3 C	5 oz

oz = ounces   C = ½ pint cups

8

Lunch can include foods from each group on the pyramid. Eat a sandwich with bread from the grain group and cheese from the dairy group. Eat this with a bowl of vegetable and bean soup. All these foods contain some fat. Add grapes to make your meal complete. Choosing good foods will help you feel strong and healthy.

This lunch has foods from each group on the pyramid. It is healthy, tasty, and easy to make.

Lunch Foods and Nutrition

All food contains **nutrients**. Some nutrients you need to be healthy are water, **carbohydrates, proteins, fats, vitamins, and minerals**. These nutrients help your body in different ways.

Carbohydrates give you **energy** to play and learn. Your body uses protein to grow and to repair injuries. Fats provide energy that can be stored to use later.

Which Lunch Foods Give You These Nutrients?

Carbohydrates

Proteins

Fats

Vitamins are needed by every part of your body. They keep your skin and eyes healthy and make your immune system strong. Your **immune system** helps you get better when you are sick or injured, and prevents you getting ill.

Minerals, like calcium and phosphorus, are used by your body to build strong bones and teeth. Minerals also help your blood and nerves to work.

vitamin A
vitamin B
potassium

Fresh vegetables, like tomatoes, are packed with nutrients. Your body needs these to stay healthy and grow.

Vitamins and Minerals Needed for a Healthy Body

vitamins: A, B group, C, D, E, and K
minerals: calcium, potassium, iron, magnesium, phosphorus, and zinc.

minerals and water

Healthy Grains for Lunch

Your body needs 6 oz (ounces) of grains every day

Grains have the biggest part of the **food pyramid** because they are the best foods to give your body **carbohydrates**. You need these for energy.

Grains also contain **vitamins**, **minerals**, and **fiber**. Foods with fiber help your body use vitamins and minerals. Fiber also makes you feel full for a longer time, and helps remove waste from your body.

You need several servings of grains every day as part of a healthy **diet**.

Pastas are made of flours from grains. They contain carbohydrates that give you energy for a long time.

Lunch Around the World

In Japan, kids sometimes eat triangle-shaped rice cakes for lunch. On the outside they are crisp. On the inside they can be filled with fish for a surprise in each bite.

All grains are seeds of plants, but some are better for you than others. **Whole grains** are healthier to eat than refined grains. Refined grains have had some of the **nutrients**, like fiber, removed.

You can eat whole grain corn, wheat, rice, or oats for lunch. These grains are made into foods like bread, tortillas, pasta, rice cakes, and crackers.

Foods made from grains come in many shapes and sizes. Are there any here that you haven't tried yet?

13

Healthy Vegetables for Lunch

Vegetables are loaded with the **nutrients** you need for good health. They give your body **vitamins, minerals, carbohydrates,** and **fiber**. A good **diet** includes vegetables every day.

Salads provide lots of different vitamins and minerals.

Eating fresh vegetables in a **whole grain** veggie wrap or sandwich is a tasty way to get good nutrition for lunch.

Veggie Wrap

Always ask an adult for help in the kitchen.

1. Spread a tortilla with cream cheese.
2. Put avocado, cucumber, and tomato onto one half.
3. Place four leaves of lettuce on the tomato.
4. Sprinkle with crunchy alfalfa sprouts or chopped onion.
5. Roll up firmly.

Vegetables give you a variety of vitamins and minerals. Eat many different kinds for a healthy diet.

15

Healthy Fruits for Lunch

Your body needs 1 1/2 C (cups) of fruit every day.

Fruits are another type of food that you need to eat every day for good health. They are high in **fiber** and have many **vitamins** and **minerals**. Fruits are the best way to get vitamin C for a healthy **immune system**. Eating fruit for lunch also gives your body **carbohydrates** for a quick boost of **energy**.

Watermelon has no fat and is high in fiber and vitamins A and C. It also has the mineral potassium. One more slice, please!

Fruits like cantaloupe, pineapple, cherries, plums, and raspberries are for sale at your local store. If you can't find your favorite fruit fresh, try to buy it frozen, rather than canned. Canned fruit sometimes has **nutrients** removed and extra sugar added.

Most stores have a wide variety of fresh fruits any time of the year.

Lunch Around the World

India grows more bananas than any other country in the world. Some bananas are sliced and fried to make banana wafers. Some children in India like to eat banana wafers with their lunch.

Healthy Dairy Foods for Lunch

Your body needs 3 C (cups) of dairy foods every day.

Milk and the foods made from milk are in the dairy group. Dairy foods give your body **protein, vitamins, minerals**, and **fats**. You need protein to grow, and heal injuries.

Dairy food has vitamin D and the minerals calcium, phosphorus, and magnesium. These help your bones and teeth grow and get strong.

A glass of milk is a good source of calcium. Low fat milk is best for you.

Dairy foods can be made with many kinds of milk. Different people around the world drink the milk from cows, goats, sheep, horses, camels, reindeer, and water buffalo. All these milks are healthy because they contain calcium and protein. Foods such as butter, cream, and cheese have the same **nutrients** as the milk they are made from.

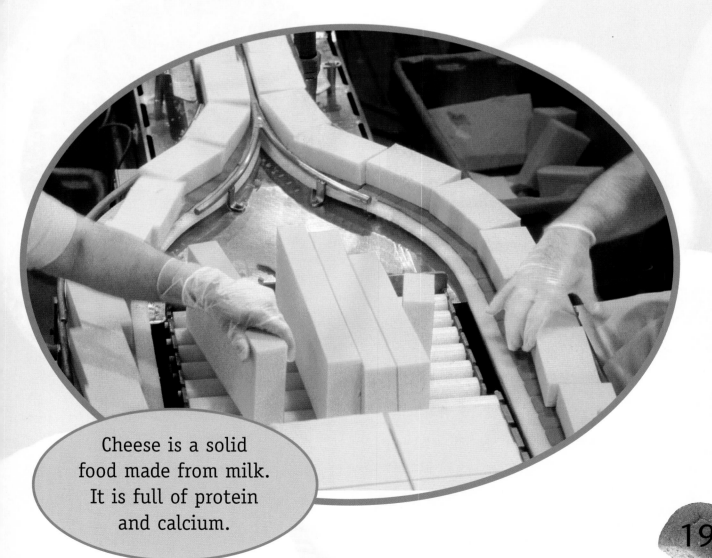

Cheese is a solid food made from milk. It is full of protein and calcium.

Healthy Meat and Beans for Lunch

Your body needs 5 oz (ounces) of meat and beans every day.

The meat and beans group includes meat, fish, beans, nuts, seeds, and eggs. These foods are all together because they all give you **protein**. The foods in this group also contain **minerals** and **fats**.

As your nails grow, new cells are made under the skin, and you trim off old cells when you cut your nails. Protein is needed for healthy new cells.

Everything in your body is made of tiny cells put together in different ways. Proteins are the building blocks your body uses to make new **cells**.

20

Meat supplies the protein you need but also has a lot of fats and **calories**. Choose foods from this group that are lower in fats for a healthier **diet**.

3oz lean hamburger
+ 2 oz mixed grain bun
+ mustard
+ ketchup

= 369 calories and 18 grams of fat

3 oz smoked white turkey
+ 2 slices whole wheat bread
+ 2 teaspoons mayonnaise
+ 3 lettuce leaves

= 306 calories and 7.5 grams of fat

Both of these are good lunch choices, but which one has a lower amount of fat?

What to Drink with Lunch

Every part of your body needs water to work properly. You need water to sweat when you get too warm. Water keeps your skin smooth and your eyes clean. Your blood is mostly made of water, and it carries **nutrients** to every part of your body.

You need to drink plenty of pure, clean water through the day. You can also make healthy drinks with juices or milk for meal or snack times.

All vegetables have a lot of water in them. Drinking vegetable juice with lunch is a good way to get water, **vitamins**, and **minerals** in your diet.

Lunch drinks can be tasty and nutritious. Here is a recipe for a strawberry smoothie. You can make smoothies with nearly any fruit, so try making up your own recipes.

Lunchtime Strawberry Smoothie

Always ask an adult to help you in the kitchen.
C = ½ pint cups

1. Peel and slice one banana.
2. Place the banana, 1½ C frozen strawberries and 1 C apple juice into a jug.
3. Blend on high speed until smooth and pink.
4. Pour into glasses and enjoy!

Prepare a Safe Lunch

To prepare a safe lunch you must have a clean work area free of **germs**. Germs are too tiny to see, but they can make food spoil and make you sick. Always wash your hands before you begin. Clean the counter top or work area with a safe disinfectant.

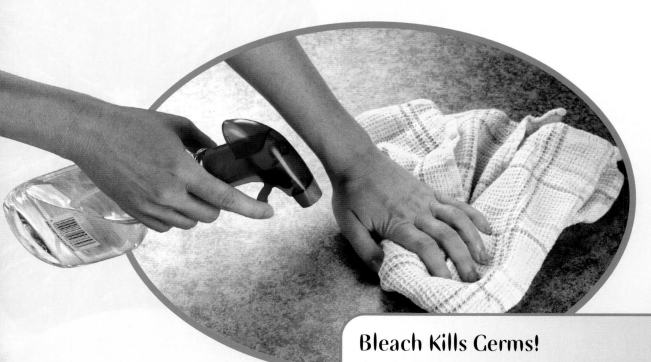

Bleach Kills Germs!

A solution of bleach and water is safe to use, and kills most germs. Ask an adult to mix one teaspoon of bleach with one quart of tap water, and put it in a clean spray bottle. Spray counter tops and wipe clean before and after preparing food.

WARNING: Keep bleach away from mouth, eyes, and skin.

Make sure that the foods you use to prepare your lunch are safe to eat. The "use by" date on a food label will tell you if food is too old. Don't use food if it looks or smells bad.

Moldy foods are not safe to eat. If you buy small amounts of fresh food and keep it cool, you can eat it all while it is still fresh.

Packing Your Lunch

You can pack your own lunch for school, a field trip, or a picnic. Start with your favorite food. Now, use the **food pyramid** to choose some foods from other groups to make a healthy meal.

Get Ready, Get Set, Pack!

Keep these items at home to help you pack a great lunch!

lunchbox ✔
zip-lock baggies ✔
thermos or juice boxes ✔
napkins ✔
small plastic box with lid ✔
plastic spoons and forks ✔
sanitizing wipes ✔
your favorite lunch foods ✔

26

Choose foods carefully for your packed lunches. Foods that don't need to stay cold, like nuts and oranges, will stay safe for many hours. Ask an adult to help you pick good foods to pack.

Easy Lunches to Pack

Lunchbox 1
cheese and ham sandwich
apple
vegetable sticks
almonds and cashews
bottled water

Lunchbox 2
chicken leg
grapes and banana
tomato
granola bar
milk in thermos

27

Lunch Planner: Mini-Pizza

preparation time:
20 minutes
cooking time:
10-15 minutes

Most people love pizza! Add your own toppings to this recipe to make your favorite lunch.

You can use any kind of flatbread to make great tasting pizza. Just add pizza sauce, vegetables and cheese.

Always ask an adult to help you in the kitchen.

Cooking utensils:
- non-stick cookie sheet
- cutting board
- sharp knife
- large spatula

Ingredients for each person:
- 1 or 2 pitta breads
- $\frac{1}{2}$ C pizza sauce
- 1 C shredded mozerella cheese
- 1 C vegetables — choose three from this list, or your favorites:
- onion
- mushrooms
- red, yellow, or green pepper
- spinach leaves

oz = ounces C = $\frac{1}{2}$ pint cups

Directions:

1. Preheat oven to 350° F (175° C).
2. Ask an adult to cut the vegetables into small pieces.
3. Place the flatbreads on a non-stick cookie sheet.
4. Spread pizza sauce over the flatbread.
5. Layer vegetables over the sauce.
6. Sprinkle grated cheese over the vegetables.
7. Cook for 10-15 minutes until slightly brown around the edges.
8. While the pizzas cook, set the table with plates, napkins, silverware, fresh fruit, and drinks of milk or water.
9. Remove pizzas from the cookie sheet and place on a cutting board.
10. Cut and serve.

Mini-pizza and fruit is a healthy lunch that you can help prepare. How many vegetables can you see on the pizza?

29

Find Out for Yourself

Choosing foods for a healthy diet is important, but it doesn't have to be difficult. Learn the basic food groups and how much you need from each one. Make good choices and enjoy good health.

Books to read

Kalman, Bobbie. *Lunch Munch*. New York: Crabtree Publishing Company, 2003.

Lobb, Janice. *Munch! Crunch! What's for Lunch?* New York: Kingfisher, 2000.

Zurakowski, Michele. *Midday Meals Around the World*. Minneapolis, MN: Picture Window Books, 2004.

Using the Internet

Explore the Internet to find out more about healthy lunch foods. Websites can change so if some of the links below no longer work, don't worry. Use a search engine, such as **www.yahooligans.com** or **www.internet4kids.com**, and type in key words such as "lunch foods," "MyPyramid," or "lunch nutrition."

Websites

www.kidshealth.org Click on "Kids site" and there are two great choices. "Staying Healthy" has information on nutrition and foods; "Recipes" offers meals that you can prepare yourself.

www.mypyramid.gov This site presents the new food pyramid with advice on how to eat the healthiest foods for your age, and the amount of daily exercise you need.

www.nutritionexplorations.org Click on "Kids site." You can learn about healthy foods, play food games, and read a new recipe.

Glossary

calorie a unit of measure of food energy

carbohydrate the part of food (such as bread and rice) that gives you energy

cell the body's smallest building block of living tissue

cooking utensils the knives, spatulas, and small tools that you use to prepare food

diet what you usually eat and drink

energy the power needed for your body to work and stay alive

fats nutrient from food (such as meat) that gives you energy

fiber material in foods (such as fruit, vegetables, and grains) that is not digested but helps carry the food through the digestive system

food pyramid a graphic that shows the food groups and daily amounts needed for a healthy diet, as recommended by the FDA (US Food and Drug Administration)

germ a small living organism that can cause disease

immune system the part of your body that protects you from disease and infection

lean meat with very little fat

mineral nutrient needed to make the body work correctly

nutrient substance (such as a vitamin, mineral, or protein) that people need to grow and stay healthy

nutrition the part of food that your body can use

protein nutrient in food that gives you energy and is used for growth and repair

vitamin nutrient in food that the body needs to stay healthy and to work correctly

whole grains grains, such as oats, wheat, corn, or rice, that have all or most of their natural fiber and nutrients

Index